the DAVIDSONS

by Archie McKerracher

SEPT NAMES INCLUDE:

Davey	Dow
Davis	Dye
Dawson	Kay
Day	Keys
Dean	MacDade
Deason	MacDavid

D1493939

the DAVIDSONS

MOTTO: Wisely if sincerely

CLAN CREST: A Stag's head

TERRITORY: Badenoch

Tartan featured on the cover is Davidson, Ancient

Published in Scotland by Lang Syne Publishers Ltd. Clydeway Centre,
45 Finnieston Street, Glasgow G3 8JU
and printed by Dave Barr Print, Glasgow.
Design by The Quick Brown Fox Company (Scotland) Limited
© Lang Syne Publishers Ltd. 1997.
I.S.B.N. 185 217 040-9

THE ORIGINS
OF THE
CLAN SYSTEM

by

RENNIE MCOWAN

The original Scottish clans of the Highlands and the great families of the Lowlands and Borders were gatherings of families, relatives, allies and neighbours for mutual protection against rivals or invaders.

Scotland experienced invasion from the

The Clan System

Vikings, the Romans and English armies from the south.

The Norman invasion of what is now England also had an influence on land-holding in Scotland. Some of these invaders stayed on and in time became 'Scottish'.

The word clan derives from the Gaelic language term 'clann', meaning children, and it was first used many centuries ago as communities were formed around tribal lands in glens and mountain fastnesses.

The format of clans changed over the centuries, but at its best the chief and his family held the land on behalf of all, like trustees, and the ordinary clansmen and women believed they had a blood relationship with the founder of their clan.

There were two way duties and obligations.

An inadequate chief could be deposed and replaced by someone of greater ability.

Clan people had an immense pride in race.

Their relationship with the chief was like adult children to a father and they had a real dignity.

The concept of clanship is very old and a more feudal notion of authority gradually crept in.

Pictland, for instance, was divided into seven principalities ruled by feudal leaders who were the strongest and most charismatic leaders of their particular groups.

By the 6th century the 'British' kingdoms of Strathclyde, Lothian and Celtic Dalriada (Argyll) had emerged and Scotland, as one nation began to take shape in the time of King Kenneth MacAlpin.

Some chiefs claimed descent from ancient kings which may not have been accurate in every case.

By the 12th and 13th centuries the clans and families were more strongly brought under the central control of Scottish monarchs.

Lands were awarded and administered more and more under royal favour, yet the power of the area clan chiefs was still very great.

The long wars to ensure Scotland's

independence against the expansionist ideas of English monarchs extended the influence of some clans and reduced the lands of others.

Those who supported Scotland's greatest king, Robert the Bruce, were awarded the territories of the families who had opposed his claim to the Scottish throne.

In the Scottish Borders country - the notorious Debatable Lands - the great families built up a ferocious reputation for providing warlike men accustomed to raiding into England and occasionally fighting one another.

Chiefs had the power to dispense justice and to confiscate lands and clan warfare produced a society where martial virtues - courage, hardiness, tenacity - were greatly admired.

Gradually the relationship between the clans and the Crown became strained as Scottish monarchs became more orientated to life in the Lowlands and, on occasions, towards England.

The Highland clans spoke a different

language, Gaelic, whereas the language of Lowland Scotland and the court was Scots and in more modern times, English.

Highlanders dressed differently, had different customs, and their wild mountain land sometimes seemed almost foreign to people living in the Lowlands.

It must be emphasised that Gaelic culture was very rich and story-telling, poetry, piping, the clarsach (harp) and other music all flourished and were greatly respected.

Highland culture was different from other parts of Scotland but it was not inferior or less sophisticated.

Central Government, whether in Edinburgh or London, sometimes saw the Gaelic clans as a challenge to their authority and some sent expeditions into the Highlands and west to crush the power of the Lords of the Isles.

Nevertheless, when the 18th century Jacobite Risings came along the cause of the Stuarts was mainly supported by Highland clans.

The Clan System

The word Jacobite comes from the Latin for James - Jacobus.

They wanted to restore the exiled Stuarts to the throne of Britain.

The monarchies of Scotland and England became one in 1603 when King James V1 of Scotland (1st of England) gained the English throne after Queen Elizabeth died.

The Union of Parliaments of Scotland and England, the Treaty of Union, took place in 1707.

Some Highland clans, of course, and Lowland families opposed the Jacobites and supported the incoming Hanoverians.

After the Jacobite cause finally went down at Culloden in 1746 a kind of ethnic cleansing took place. The power of the chiefs was curtailed.

Tartan and the pipes were banned in law.

Many emigrated, some because they wanted to, some because they were evicted by force.

In addition, many Highlanders left for

the cities of the south to seek work.

Many of the clan lands became home to sheep and deer shooting estates.

But the warlike traditions of the clans and the great Lowland and Border families lived on.

Their descendants fought bravely for freedom in two world wars.

Remember the men from whence you came, says the Gaelic proverb, and to that could be added the role of many heroic women.

The spirit of the clan, of having roots, whether Highland or Lowland, means much to thousands of people.

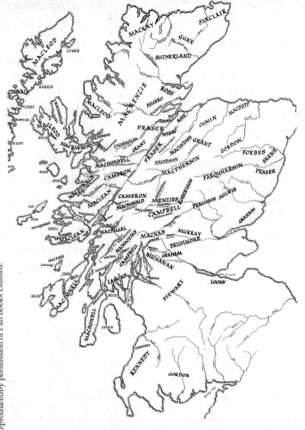

A map of the Clans Homelands.

CHAPTER ONE:
SLAUGHTER AND RESTRUCTION

The Davidsons are one of the principal branch clans of the confederation of clans which formed the mighty Clan Chattan, the Clan of the Cat. Their patrynomic is Mhic Daibhidh, or MacDaidh, son of David, for they descend from David Dhu, fourth son of Muirich, the Celtic hereditary lay prior or parson of Kingussie who was 4th Chief of Clan Chattan in the 13th century. The second son was Ewen whose patrynomic was Mhic Phearsain, son of the parson. In later years the Davidsons and MacPhersons became dire enemies despite, or perhaps because of, their close relationship.

The Davidson lands were at Invernahaven near Kingussie in Badenoch, where the rivers Truim and Spey meet, adjacent to the lands of the MacPhersons.

Both clans belonged to Clan Chattan, the Clan of the Cat, a confederation of clans who claimed as their progenitor Gilliechattan Mor who was 1st Chief of Clan Chattan in the 11th century. The original lands of old Clan Chattan were in Lochaber with the chief's castle being at Torcastle. Gillie Chattan Mor The Servant of St Catan, was descended from the Royal House of Lorn. St Catan's name means Little Cat, perhaps an affectionate pun for a revered churchman, but the heraldic beast of Clan Chattan became a snarling wild-cat with the motto "Touch not the Cat Without a Glove".

Eva, heiress of Clan Chattan, and granddaughter of Muirich the Parson, married 23-year-old Angus, 6th chief of the Mackintoshes in 1291, and brought the chieftainship and lands of Clan Chattan to him.

An old manuscript says the marriage came about because Alexander MacDonald, Lord of the Isles, sent his nephew Angus Mackintosh, Chief of the Mackintoshes, to Dugall Dall Macgilliechattan, Chief of Clan Chattan, to inform him the Lord of the Isles would pay him a visit.

Apparently it was the custom that the Lord of the Isles required to be provided with either the host's wife or daughter as a companion for the night when he came to visit. Macgilliechattan, to avoid this, managed to hastily marry his daughter Eva to Angus Mackintosh when he brought the message, and thus Angus became paramount Chief of Clan Chattan.

The centre of power of Clan Chattan now moved to the Mackintosh lands in Badenoch and there was a migration of clans people into the area from which Bruce had recently removed the Comyn family. Angus Mackintosh then rented out the extensive Clan Chattan lands in Lochaber and west Badenoch to the Camerons. However, no sooner had they taken possession than they refused to pay the stipulated rent. The Camerons then claimed the land by right of the sword, and this led to numerous minor conflicts over the next century.

The Mackintosh chiefs usually solved the matter by raiding the Cameron lands and taking cattle in lieu of money. Finally, the Camerons had had enough. They marched into Badenoch in 1375 with a huge force and stripped it bare with terrible slaughter. They were stopped at the Davidson lands of Invernahaven by Lachlan Mackintosh, 8th Chief of Clan Chattan, who had hurried south with some of his own men to take command of a force comprised of MacPhersons and Davidsons.

The two armies met at the junction of the rivers Truim and Spey south of Kingussie. The Mackintosh ordered the combined clans forward but a bitter argument broke out between the other two chiefs as to which should have the honour of commanding the right wing of Clan Chattan.

Cluny MacPherson claimed the right as senior representative on the male side of the older Clan Chattan, and Davidson said it was his as the oldest cadet family. The exasperated Mackintosh chose the Davidsons, and urged them both on. The MacPhersons, considering themselves grossly insulted, then left the field of battle and waded across the Spey. They sat on the little birch covered knoll to the north of the river junction and ate their midday meal watching the battle purely as disinterested spectators. They saw MacDaidh, the Davidson Chief, and his seven sons, killed within two hundred yards of their own house; they saw the Mackintosh line begin to waver amidst the clash of claymore on targe; they heard the whistle of arrows and the screams of dying men. But they still did not move.

Lachlan Mackintosh realised Clan Chattan was losing badly and resorted to a subterfuge. He told his bard to take a circuitous route to make it appear he had come from the Camerons, and pretend to be one of them. He was to compose and recite to the MacPhersons a satirical poem accusing them of cowardice. The office of bard was a sacred one which enabled the holder to travel freely between enemies and deliver his message without harm . Thus no one took any notice of the bard as he made his way through the two forces to the little island where the MacPhersons sat.

Pretending to come from the Camerons, the bard burst into recitation. His ballad, roughly translated, said "the false party are on the hillock, and the man with the big brown eyes (the Mackintosh) is in distress: It was not out of friendship to us, but merely your own cowardice that made you sit and watch".

The MacPhersons were enraged at supposedly being so taunted by the victor of the fight and followed the Camerons back up into the mountains. Here they fell upon them with dreadful slaughter, and killed their chief Charles Macalonair at a hollow in the hills beside Loch Pataig, henceforth known as Coire Thearlaich, Charlie's Cauldron.

The clash of sword and spear.

CHAPTER TWO:
PROPHECIES AND PERSONALITIES

Later the name almost vanishes from Badenoch, being replaced by the names of MacPhersons and Mackintoshes. A manu-script by Lachlan Shaw says the Invernahaven family changed their name to MacPherson by decision of their chief Seumas Laggach. An alternative account suggests that in 1524 Milmoir MacDaidh murdered Lachlan, 14th chief of the Mackintoshes, who had ruined his hopes of marrying a rich widow.

For this crime he and another Davidson were held prisoner in Loch an Eilean castle for seven years without trial, then tortured, hanged and beheaded. Perhaps it was the shame of this that led the Davidsons to assume the name of their closest kin as they too were "sons of the parson".

There is certainly no mention of them in the list of broken clans of "the haill kin

A Davidson was held prisoner for seven years without trial, then tortured, hanged and beheaded.

of Clann Chattan" compiled in the mid-16th century. Nor are they found in the list of those attending the great gathering of Clan Chattan at Termit in Petty near Inverness in 1609, although the old records do state there were others of Clan Muirich from Badenoch as well as "Cluny MacFersone".

However, it appears possible that a survivor of the chief's family, and a few followers, left Speyside and made their way to the north east. The next firm record is of Donald Davidson who acquired land at Davidston near Cromarty around the middle of the 17th century. He claimed descent from an ancestor who had entered the service of the King of France and was recorded in 1629 in the "Livre d'Or" as one who could trace noble birth through six generations.

His son became town clerk of the county while his grandson William married in 1719 the daughter of the Bayne laird who owned the estate of Tulloch at

Dingwall. Their son Henry Davidson, born in 1729, made his way to London and amassed a fortune in the West Indies trade. He returned north in 1763 and bought Tulloch for £10,500 from his Bayne in-laws, and this became the seat of the Davidson chiefs from then on.

By virtue of this ownership they also became Keepers of the Royal Castle of Dingwall, although by this time it was pretty ruinous. His brother Duncan, a lawyer, succeeded him in 1781 and made great improvements to the estate. He also built the main road north from Dingwall and reclaimed land from the sea. He was a Member of Parliament for Cromarty from 1790 to 1796. His son Henry, another prosperous West Indies merchant, succeeded him and also carried out tree plantings and improvements.

Tulloch Castle was by this time a crumbling ruin. It had been built originally in 1166 on Tulloch Hill at the north end of Dingwall and rebuilt by the Munros in

1400, and was a Barony held by right of the Crown. It was gradually added to over the years. The Exchequer Rolls of 1608 describe Tulloch as the most important castle in the north in the reign of James 1V, commanding Ross, Sutherland and Caithness. It was said to be the strongest castle north of Stirling and an inventory in the 17th century describes it containing 17 beds, 10 feather beds,14 brazen candlesticks, 80 lbs weight of pewter, 9 tables, 18 vats of fish, 14 hogsheads of wine, 4 great guns, and one long range cannon.

The castle was so ruinous and its upkeep so great that Henry Davidson leased it to the Rev Colin McKenzie to turn into a factory. Nothing came of this but many of the castle's carved stones found their way into the walls of the minister's farm buildings. Tulloch Castle was badly damaged in a fire of 1845.

Duncan Davidson, 4th laird of Tulloch, was born in 1800 and became Member of Parliament for Cromarty in

1826. He rebuilt Tulloch Castle in a more modern style in 1853. He was a great favourite of Queen Victoria and was her Lord Lieutenant for Ross and Cromarty. She summoned him to drive her personally on her visits north, possibly admiring his handsome and imposing appearance. Certainly, he made a dramatic figure on the driving seat of her carriage, being dressed in full Highland garb with his long white hair flowing over his shoulders.

However, he was also known locally as The Stag, a play both on his armorial insignia and his sexual prowess, having had five wives who bore him eighteen children, while he had fathered at least thirty illegitimate children around the district.

One of his wives was the youngest sister of his daughter in law. He is also remembered for being the subject of one of the Brahan Seer's famous predictions - "The day will come when there will be a Laird of Tulloch who will kill four wives in

The Brahan Seer who predicted "the day will come when there will be a Laird of Tulloch who will kill four wives in succession, but the fifth will kill him."

succession, but the fifth will kill him".

Interestingly, Duncan died of pneumonia in Edinburgh after attending the famous Wet Review of Volunteers by Queen Victoria at Holyrood in 1881. Being summoned to stand beside the queen's carriage he insisted on remaining bare headed in the pouring rain despite her entreaties to put his cap on. He replied that a Highland gentleman should always remain uncovered in his sovereign's presence. This chivalrous gesture led to his death and, just as the Brahan Seer predicted, his fifth wife survived him.

There is another interesting connection here because Duncan Davidson was a frequent visitor to nearby Brahan Castle, seat of the Earls of Seaforth, Chiefs of Clan McKenzie. He had heard many of the predictions about this family being discussed by them around the dinner table, and lived to see them fulfilled.

The most famous of these was "There will be four great lairds in the days of the deaf and dumb Seaforth – Gairloch; Chisholm; Lovat; and Raasay. One of them will be buck- toothed, another hare-lipped, another half-witted, and the fourth a stammerer . . . when he (Seaforth) looks around and sees them he will know his sons are doomed, his broad lands shall pass to strangers, and his race shall come to an end. And of the great House of Brahan not a stone shall remain".

It is a fact that Francis McKenzie, born 1755, heir to the Earldom of Seaforth, became deaf and dumb due to an infection while at school at Eton. When he became Earl his contemporaries were the buck-toothed McKenzie laird of Gairloch; the simple minded Fraser of Lovat; the hear lipped Chishilm of Chisholm; and McLeod of Raasay who had a speech impediment.

Francis McKenzie later had four sons who all died young. The estates were sold and the line of McKenzies of Kintail came to an end. Brahan Castle was demolished after the Second World War and not a trace remains. The interesting fact is that Duncan Davidson had made a note of all these predictions after hearing them discussed and personally witnessed them being fulfilled.

His grandson Duncan, born 1865, became 6th Laird of Tulloch in 1889. He could not afford to live in Tulloch Castle in appropriate style, nor maintain it, and leased it out. He moved to Hampshire from where he commuted to London. His health broke down after fourteen years working as a West Indian merchant and he returned to Tulloch Castle, although apparently staying with his mother in more modest accomodation in the castle grounds. He took a keen interest in local affairs, being a judge of the piping and dancing at the Inverness Games; a Sheriff Substitute; County Commissioner of Scouts; and Deputy Lord Lieutenant.

He was also keenly interested in clan affairs and in 1909 he called a meeting of

Davidsons in London to form a Clan Society. It was proposed and carried that Davidson of Tulloch should be elected as Chief of the Davidsons. This caused some controversy but in fact, the Davidsons of Tulloch had been recognised as the Chiefs of that name by most historians over the previous century, including Lord Lyon.

Duncan Davidson died in 1917 without leaving an heir and he nominated as his successor Mrs Douglas Vickers, a distant kinswoman through the female line who did not take up the Arms. She extensively restored Tulloch Castle in 1925 to designs by the famous architect Robert Lorimer.

Her son Angus Vickers became 7th of Tulloch, (but not of Davidson), and sold Tulloch Castle in recent years to Ross and Cromarty County Council. The castle and its policies are now encroached on by modern housing estates and after being used by Highland Region for scholastic purposes is now an hotel.

The chieftainship of Clan Davidson became dormant after the death of Duncan Davidson and the Clan Society he founded ceased functioning in 1939.

The other principal Davidson cadet families were Davidsons of Cantray near Culloden which was held by them for nearly two hundred years; and Davidson of Inchmarlo.

Sir Robert Davidson, Lord Provost of Aberdeen, is remembered for his fearless action in leading out the townsfolk to repel an army of Islanders led by the Lord of the Isles at the bloody battle of Harlaw in 1411. Sir Robert was killed and his suit of armour is still preserved in Aberdeen Council Chambers.

Another notable clan member was Sir William Davidson, born in Dundee in 1615, who became a merchant in Amsterdam. Cromwell had forbidden imports in foreign vessels so William had the ownership of several Dutch ships transferred to him and made a fortune. On behalf of the exiled King Charles 11 he sent 10,000 guilders worth of arms to the Royalist general Middleton, but only received a tiny percentage back after the Restoration. In recompense the king made him a baronet and agent for England and Ireland in the Low Countries. He was also made Conservator of Scots Privileges. His portrait hangs in the National Portrait Gallery in Edinburgh.

The Clan Davidson Association was revived in 1991 and publishes a regular magazine on clan affairs. In the same year Duncan Hector Davidson J.P. of New Zealand became Heir in Law to the Chieftainship, tracing his descent from Hector Francis Duncan (1857-1907), fourth son of the 4th laird of Tulloch. His claim to the dormant chieftainship is being considered by the Lord Lyon at the time of writing.

But in Badenoch only a few crumbling stones mark the site of the house of Invernahaven on the clan lands which the early Davidsons fought so bravely to defend in that dreadful battle in 1375, and in doing so nearly removed themselves from the pages of history.

A Davidson Clansman in battle.

Highland Weapons

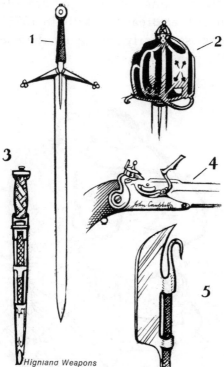

Highland Weapons
1. The Claymore or two-handed sword (Fifteenth or early Sixteenth century)
2. Basket hilt of Broadsword made in Stirling, 1716
3. Highland Dirk — Eighteenth century
4. Steel Pistol (detail) made in Doune
5. Head of Lochaber Axe as carried in the '45 and earlier.